This book belongs to

....

....

....

Made in the USA
Monee, IL
23 November 2022

18400129R00063